T0128883

Just a Spoonful of Laughter Helps the Medicine Go Down

A series of short stories that will make you laugh, maybe even cry, and hopefully make me a lot of money.

Richard D. Edgerly, MD

Illustrated by Frederick W. Porter

WestBow
PRESS
A DIVISION OF THOMAS NELSON

WestBow Press books may be ordered through booksellers or by contacting:

WestBow Press
A Division of Thomas Nelson
1663 Liberty Drive
Bloomington, IN 47403
www.westbowpress.com
1-(866) 928-1240

Because of the dynamic nature of the Internet, any Web addresses or links contained in this book may have changed since publication and may no longer be valid. The views expressed in this work are solely those of the author and do not necessarily reflect the views of the publisher, and the publisher hereby disclaims any responsibility for them.

Any people depicted in stock imagery provided by Thinkstock are models, and such images are being used for illustrative purposes only.

Certain stock imagery © Thinkstock.

ISBN: 978-1-4497-1011-8 (sc)
ISBN: 978-1-4497-1012-5 (dj)
ISBN: 978-1-4497-1010-1 (e)

Library of Congress Control Number: 2010942202

Printed in the United States of America

WestBow Press rev. date: 03/24/2011

Contents

Introduction

Some of you may remember the book, movie, or even the television series named "All Creatures Great and Small." They depicted the office experiences of British veterinary physician Alf Wight (penned under the name James Herriot).

Similarly, this book is about true, although perhaps slightly embellished for readability, stories of events that happened either in my own medical practice or in those of a close associate or two.

However, I can't imagine anyone ever wanting to make a movie or television series from any of these stories, but who knows? We do have reality TV these days.

Regardless, I hope you enjoy reading them as much as I enjoyed remembering and writing them down. I hope they allow you to peer into the life of a physician for just a little while to experience some of the things that they see and feel on a daily basis. If not, then at least they should be enjoyable enough to qualify for "bathroom reading." Perhaps they will at least allow you to spend a few more minutes in the bathroom and promote a little better bowel movement. Enjoy!

Dr. Richard Edgerly, MD

Dedication

To my lovely wife Lori, I dedicate this book. She always wanted to be the wife of a physician. Unfortunately, she thought I said I *was* a physician when I meant that I *wanted* to be one. Thanks for graciously putting me through medical school, even donating your plasma to pay the bills. And thank you for raising our three wonderful children. Sorry if that made you lose your mind.

To my daughter Jocelyn, for still laughing at all my stupid jokes, even after all these years. Thank you for inspiring me to be more Christ-like and sharing the humor we find in even the littlest of things. And thank you for allowing me to pass them on to our wonderful grandchild. Get ready Howie. Your fearlessness to pursue any goal is not only admirable but a testimony to your trust in our Lord's Sovereignty and Omnipotence.

To my daughter Holly, whose sharp wit makes *me* laugh. Thank you for editing this book and for keeping me on my toes as we rip people apart when they do things that are stupid, behind their backs of course. Your drive to be the best at what you do, and your willingness to heal the broken people of the world, is spiritually an inspiration to me.

To my son Drew, the most patient man I know. Sometimes, you must think that the rest of us in the family are absolutely nuts. Thanks for not saying so. I admire your wisdom and the love you have for people. When I grow up, I want to be just like you.

To my son-in-law Jason, for keeping me on the edge of the latest technology, kicking and screaming all the way. Thanks for tolerating my type-A personality and the warp speed I use to get things done, even if they are completely in the wrong direction. And thank you for loving Jocelyn and Howie.

To my son-in-law Fred, for not only doing the illustrations in this book, but also for having a truly humble, honest and child-like spirit. You're refreshing! Thank you for loving Holly.

To Billie, my faithful nurse. Thank you for working with me when you could be working with anyone else in the world.

And to my three medical partners: Dr. Steve Taylor MD, Dr. Joe Vickers MD, and Dr. Craig Whittlesey MD. Thank you keeping me around and keeping us together through thick and thin. All for one and one for all—not in the money department, of course.

I love you guys.

Quincy

This is a true story. Believe it or not, it is not even embellished. Well, not much anyway.

Before I became a physician, I had the privilege of majoring in Bacteriology and Public Health from Washington State University. Go Cougs! That propelled me into a career of laboratory medicine which I enjoyed *tremendously*. The latter half of that career was spent in Pathology, which turned out to be a dead end job, if you get my drift. Although it was fascinating, we performed the autopsies for the county which was not something you wrote home about.

One funny part of this story is I am a Caucasian and found myself working as a laboratory assistant for a first generation Chinese Pathologist. It was the mirror image of Dr. Quincy and his laboratory assistant Sam, for those of you who might remember that television series. Anyway, I find it appropriate to mention this tidbit as it really adds to the story.

On this particular day, Sam and I, or would that be Dr. Quincy and I, were asked to perform an autopsy on a man that had been "burned beyond recognition." They were right. I didn't recognize him but I may have seen him once on a barbeque before I learned there is a low heat mode. It was not a good day to work in the Pathology department and

I, unfortunately, had asked my wife to lunch that day before I knew our assignment. It wasn't a good day for lunch either.

This unfortunate man had owned a mobile home that he had positioned way out of town. We all know the reputation of mobile homes for being fire starters and it proved true here. In addition, when you are "way out of town" nobody can rescue you from the inferno. And, no one had. His remains were basically charred meat in the rough shape of a human skeleton. Even his limbs had been burned off as they were the thinnest places of his body, just as with you and me, I assume. No feet, no hands, just a torso and a left arm were left, and a charcoal one at that. We figured he must have been lying on his left arm, as it showed just enough skin to show that he was at least wearing a watch at the time of his unfortunate demise.

As forensic pathologists, we were to determine when he died and whether he died of "foul play" or not. In other words, did someone stab or shoot him first and then torch his place to cover up a murder or was he just a smoker that fell asleep? After thorough investigation, we did not find any foul play. But the interesting part was finding out *when* he died.

Trying to be a top notch pathologist assistant, or perhaps just a bit weird, I suggested that we try to find the watch that had left its impression on his left arm. After a thorough search we did just that. How unbelievable that we would find his watch after such a horrible fire. We hoped that we would find out exactly when he died if we were lucky enough to have a watch that not only had the hands but also a calendar piece. We were so excited after the find that we could hardly wait to examine it. After wiping off the soot with a rag, I laughed for the rest of the day. That's right. It was a Timex and it was still ticking! I could just picture John Cameron Swayze holding up this man's charred arm during a commercial on national television, saying, "Timex, it takes a licking and keeps on ticking."

Dodge Ball

In the practice of medicine there is one thing you must learn to do if you are going to survive: Dodge all body fluids. This may sound easy but unfortunately it is not and you often learn the hard way. It starts as a first year medical student. You first learn that they can come at you from any angle, get by any barrier, and that your position in the fray increases your net exposure. Because you are the scab, scum, or whatever you call the lowest man on the totem pole, it isn't until later in your medical career that you learn to anticipate them. By that time, you can also get the medical student training under you to act as the shield instead.

Occasionally, even the pros still get hit. One incident I remember the most was when I was training in my emergency medicine rotation. This is usually a couple of months long, seven days a week, and twelve hours per day. At least it is shift work, as we say, and that means no after-hours call. You know when you start, when you finish, and when you get to sleep. It was wonderful for these reasons and the fun of seeing all kinds of trauma and real action made it, well, fun.

I was working the late shift when a patient presented with a pilonidal cyst. These are in the lower area of the back and can get quite large. I wasn't a rookie by this time, so I was pretty comfortable giving the anesthesia and proceeding with the incision and drainage. These can be several inches long and unfortunately, several inches deep. Oh, also, and most importantly, abscesses are under a tremendous amount of pressure which is why they are usually so painful. Once you relieve the pressure, the pain subsides.

Unfortunately, the emergency room physician wasn't as comfortable with me doing the procedure as I was with my own skills. He made me call the general surgeon on-call to come in and do the procedure or at least supervise. I had actually trained under the general surgeon a year earlier and he was confident that I had the skills to perform the procedure unassisted. Plus, he was on his way to a Christmas party. But the emergency room physician wasn't caving in. The general surgeon finally agreed to drop by and supervise the procedure. To make his trip to the party quicker, I had the patient prepped and ready upon his arrival. Unfortunately, when I made the opening incision, the contents under pressure found their way onto the general surgeon and his fancy party shirt. Oops. He was now covered in pus and had to return home to change his shirt. He made sure to give the ER physician a few choice words on his way out about where he was on that totem pole I spoke of earlier.

An even better incident yet, was one that happened to one of my partners. He was delivering a baby and had taken the time to change into the best protective garb available to mankind. He was covered properly from head to toe and even took the extra precaution of wearing a surgical mask, shield included. There was no way he would get soiled, or so he thought. Here came the baby along with all the usual fluids under pressure that are backed up behind the pressure plug known as the babies head. Fluid went everywhere. And I mean everywhere. It even cleared that mask with the shield. All he told me was, "Amniotic fluid is very salty." Yuk!

A Formal Education

My personal history includes the fact that I am the product of two wonderful parents. However, it also includes the fact that they were not highly educated. Or so I occasionally thought. My father finished high school, and as most young men his age, he joined the service of his country at the start of WWII and completed a tour of duty in the Army Air Force. Mom, on the other hand, finished her educational career in junior high. She thought about high school but when they wouldn't let her participate in art class where she was especially gifted, she bailed. She always regretted that.

I was the fifth of six children. My parents strived to have the perfect child and finally on the fifth try, they succeeded. Why they continued to have a sixth child we will never know. It was probably a mistake. Just ask the other five of us.

I was the first child to go on to college. School always came easily to me and after high school, I worked my way through Washington State University where I received my Bachelor of Science degree in Bacteriology and Public Health. Please don't ask to see my transcripts. I was then fortunate enough to complete medical school at the University of Washington where I fulfilled my childhood dream of becoming a doctor of medicine. After all of this education, I learned that you don't have to go to college to become educated. In fact, at times, it may even be a hindrance.

For example, I was sitting in my office one day wrestling with a sandscape that someone had given to me for graduation. You remember sandscapes, the entirely mind-numbing desk ornaments composed of sand and oil pressed between two sheets of glass and enclosed in a wooden frame? Each time you turn the frame over, a new and beautiful sandscape picture would form. Mine sucked. It stopped making pictures at all because it had filled with air that quickly put its usefulness to a stand still.

Being well educated of course, I got the idea of using a needle and syringe to withdraw the air that created the annoying vacuum problem. It worked for a short while before filling again. Darn! I then decided to use the needle and syringe again but this time I sealed the hole left by the needle with chewing gum. Again, there was seeming success, but only for a limited while. Enter my uneducated mother.

After watching me with another futile attempt, she looked at me and asked if I had ever learned anything about fluid dynamics while I was receiving all this education. She informed me that the sandscape problem would only be resolved if I was to inject fluid *into* the apparatus. Only then would I overcome the vacuum created by the air with the oil and sand mixture. She completed the lesson by informing me, "I may not be well educated but I at least have horse sense." I knew better than to ask her what that was.

A Tale of Two Technologies

"It was the best of times, it was the worst of times…" So starts the novel, *A Tale of Two Cities*. Many of us have read and enjoyed this story of contrast between London and Paris, occurring I believe, in the eighteenth century. That famous opening line reminds me of the dilemma many of us face as physicians as we advance in the world of technology. We have at our fingertips the best of the information superhighway. We can access the latest in medical research, literally, as it leaves the experimental laboratory. There is information readily available from some of the finest medical research institutions in the world. Unfortunately, those who search that technology also have access to some of the worst. And few that read these findings can actually discern the difference. In medical school, we are actually taught how to tell the difference between good and bad studies, which is necessary at times, as we race down that information superhighway at breakneck speed.

The Bible says that at the end times there will be wars and rumors of wars. Well, the same phenomenon exists in medical literature. Today, thanks to junk science, cures and rumors of cures inundate the Internet, newspapers, and all other transmittable resources. And they are able to put this information, and many times misinformation, into the hands of our patients faster than we can get them critically evaluated. I can't tell you how many times I have heard patients tell me things that rival all the "olde wives' tales" we have already heard and disparaged from the ancients.

"Say Doc, they say that if you drink a little vinegar mixed with sea salt as you suck on a sweet pickle while driving east on highway 410 on the odd days of the week, you won't get cancer and you'll never have to go to the physician again."

I answer back, "Where did you hear that?"

"I read it on the Internet," he retorts.

"Then I suggest that you do it.

Now, put that information superhighway into the hands of a hypochondriac and you really have a dilemma. That's exactly what happened to one of my medical partners. One of his "worried well" patients unfortunately had access to all that same information on the same information superhighway. She had been perusing the literature as soon as it was released from the research mice themselves and came to him convinced that she finally knew what was wrong with her. She had the exact same symptoms listed as the literature described and was anxious to tell him and start down the road to recovery. She wanted to feel good, relieve her symptoms, and never have to visit her doctor again.

When he asked her what she had, she gave him the definitive diagnosis as discerned through all her search of the literature available. She was convinced that she had prostate cancer (by the way, women do not have prostates just as men do not have uteruses). So, as you travel down that information highway, remember what the state patrol always reminds us: speed kills.

An Eight Year Old Dad?

There are very few miracles in medicine. Yes, there are a lot of heroics. And yes, there are amazing stories that have been passed down from one generation of physicians to another. Then there are stories like this one that deserve to be told because they come along only once or so in a career.

When I graduated from my Family Medicine Residency and began delivering babies, I knew that I would experience a lot. And I did. I saw thirteen year-old mothers and twenty-six year-old grandmothers. But I never thought that I would ever see an eight year-old father.

Mark and his wife came to see me when they first discovered that they were pregnant. They seemed responsible. They were a delight to see in the office. They liked me and I liked them. I was also proud to be a part of the experience when I was called to the obstetrical unit to help his wife when she came into the hospital in active labor. It was to be a special moment for the three of us, those two especially.

Irma performed like a champ, as she patiently waited for her cervix to dilate to ten centimeters. She began pushing with all the vim and vigor anyone could expect. She and her husband worked together and waited with the anticipation of bringing a new baby into the world and starting a new extension of their family.

And here she came. She delivered without incident and this eight year-old man became a father on his own birthday. That's right, February 29th 2004. Now what are the odds of that happening? WOW!

Dementia, the Mind is a Terrible Thing to Waste.

After you graduate from medical school and residency, it is time to begin your private practice, ready or not. I remember starting out with very few patients. I had all day to talk to just a few. My salary was guaranteed for the first year as I established my clientele and it was wonderful. Now, I am forced to rush from patient to patient and time to visit must actually be calculated in. The key is finding the right balance and I hope I am doing just that. Many still come to see me so perhaps I am.

On the first day, I was informed that I had just inherited a batch of nursing home patients that had been under the care of a physician who had been there before me. Having plenty of open space on my schedule, I asked if each patient could be brought over to my clinic which was just next door. They were happy to oblige.

Patient number one was Mr. Jones. He had been a patient at the home for several years and seemed to be one of the happiest people in the world. He answered every question with a grin on his face and a hardy, "Yep, yep, yep." I went over his entire medical record for the next half an hour. What a wonderful time we had. And then something happened. I *asked* him a question instead of just regurgitating his medical history.

I asked him if he could tell me the name of the President of the United States. "Yep, yep, yep." I asked him if he knew the current day of the week. "Yep, yep, yep." I asked him where he lived. Again, "Yep, yep, yep." Boy, had I been an idiot. Mr. Jones had *severe* dementia and I might as well have spent half an hour talking to a post.

It was about this time that my nurse walked into the room to see if she could assist. I decided to have a little fun, taking advantage of what I had just learned. In front of her, I asked him, Did you assassinate John F. Kennedy? "Yep, yep, yep" Boy was my nurse startled. I explained how stupid I had been and we all learned a lesson that day.

My second patient was from the same nursing home. She had a history of recurrent urinary tract infections and was experiencing one now. This is a common thing in the elderly as their urinary tract ages and they are unable to empty the bladder as readily as they did when they were younger. Subsequently, the urine stagnates and easily colonizes the available bacteria there.

My nurse then made the mistake of asking me why elderly women always seem to struggle with these infections. I told her that it was because they were still sexually active. Startled a bit, she asked, "With whom?" I told her, "Mr. Jones." I had just asked him a minute ago and he had said, "Yep, yep, yep."

"Did I Do That?"

We can all remember Steve Erkle making famous this old line. We would hear it right after some catastrophe occurred on the set where Steve was the obvious source. He would look around with those silly glasses of his, snort and ask, "Did I do that?" It always brought a great laugh around our house. Well, sometimes in medicine, our mishaps may not be that funny.

Mishaps are not as unusual around the doctor's office as one might hope. With any action there is always a reaction. And as much as I like to believe I am in control, I AM NOT. However, we are pretty good at covering them up, I assure you. This is why we call it the *practice* of medicine. If this bothers you, then don't come to the doctor's office. Die of your colon cancer or heart disease and suffer through your hemorrhoids without me. But if you want honest help to relieve pain and suffering or help avoiding the big catastrophes that may threaten your life, I am here for you. I will do the very best I can. However, there are no guarantees. Otherwise, life is a risk, and not always a calculated one, of course.

One catastrophe occurred early in my medical practice. This is when they should occur by the way. Then we learn from our mistakes and become better physicians. We always want to be better physicians next year than we are this year. This is referred to as "trial and error." To learn from other people's mistakes is called "a formal education." We do that too. This one, I unfortunately learned on my own.

Many children are plagued by recurrent ear infections. If not the ones that cause fever, ear pulling, and crying all through the night, they can also be "serous otitis" that just results in a continuous plugging of the ear that hinders hearing and if not corrected, eventually speech. These are the children that we refer to the otolaryngologists who are happy to place the myringotomy tubes to relieve the fluid and pressure. You may know them as the "ear, nose, and throat" doctor. Doesn't otolaryngologists sound so much smarter?

I was asked to see Jimmy this day for the same. He had recently had an upper respiratory infection with the usual runny nose, cough, and general malaise. His mom had had enough and wanted to make sure his ears were not infected again. He had been to the otolaryngologist earlier in his life and had tubes put in. They had done their job until now she thought. After looking carefully at Jimmy, I concluded that they certainly had. I was able to visualize the tympanic membrane fairly well and at least on the left side the tube was, in fact, still there doing the job we had asked it to do. The tube on the right was different. It appeared to me that it had worked its way out and was now just lying there in the external canal. This is also what we expect them to do after a year or so. No problem, the tympanic membrane actually causes this and then closes up right behind it. It is a wonderful process. Isn't the body created amazingly? Usually the tube eventually falls out in the bathtub somewhere and no one ever sees it. Sometimes they just lie there in the external canal waiting for a young inexperienced physician to see it, pluck it out, and charge a "removal of foreign body" fee, although that should never be the reason for doing the procedure.

After examining Jimmy, I asked mom how long ago he had the tubes put in because this one appeared to be serving no purpose and I would be happy to pluck it out with my little alligator clips. "Oh, a long time," I was told. Eager to please and inexperienced enough not to know the difference, I did just that. Unfortunately, I heard a loud "pop" as the tube came out of the tympanic membrane and blood oozed out as a result. I had just undone a one hour surgery in one second. "How long ago were those tubes placed?" I again asked. "Oh, about three months ago," she replied.

"Did I do that?" I covered up my mistake by assuring mom that I thought his ear would drain just fine. It should, since there was a nice hole there now.

Did You Just Say What I Thought You Said?

One of the most important things about *working* in medicine is the need to know the *language* of medicine. It's not that we try to make things difficult or try to make ourselves seem so important that we sit around at night making up big names for body parts, really. And we surely don't try to do this when we are on call and have been without sleep for two days, although it may seem so. When "modern medicine" was being developed, Latin was the common language for most scientists of the day. And many of them may have been *mad* scientists, by the way. Who else would steal bodies under the cover of darkness and dissect them in order to identify and name every muscle, bone, nerve and artery?

So, it's important to spend some of your time during medical school looking up word derivations that explain what is really going on. For example, when we are learning anatomy, we look at the Latin word and the rest may be self-explanatory. What is the **fossa ovale**? It is an *oval hole* that exists in the heart of an infant prior to birth because the blood needs to be shunted from the right atrium to the left atrium without going through the lungs. Remembering that the baby doesn't use its lungs prior to taking that famous first breath helps us remember why that hole is important. It closes, of course, once the baby takes that breath and the physiology of oxygenation changes outside of the womb. This is why they used to hold the baby upside down and spank it on the butt right after it was delivered. It was not just because the doctor was angry for having to get up in the middle of the night, although having been there, that sometimes felt like the right thing to do. We don't do that anymore because someone invented the video camera, and on film, that just looks bad. How fair is that?

For another example, if you hear a physician say that he thinks the patient's problem is supra*tentorial*, it means that we think that it is all in their head. Anatomically, there is a "tent" (the tentorium) of tissue that separates the brain from the structures beneath it and knowing this gives us the derivation of the word. If you hear the doctor say this about *you* when he thinks the door is closed and it isn't, then you may want to find yourself another doctor, and right away.

Not knowing this special language and yet trying to use it has also been known to bring in a few laughs. One of my medical partners who is still delivering babies (speaking of mad scientists by the way) sent his very pregnant patient to the laboratory for some much needed blood work. She was nearing her EDC (estimated date of confinement), or what people commonly refer to as the "due date," and her belly showed it.

The lab tech asked, "When are you going to deliver?" She answered back, "If I don't deliver by this weekend, my doctor is going to *seduce* me." He swears that he told her *induce* and has denied any and all other allegations of course!

N. E. S. T. L. E. S.
Nestles Makes the Very Best, Chocolate.

It was a hot summer day, I remember. I remember that because, shortly before this next office visit, I had noticed that the chocolate covered peanuts I had stored in my pickup truck for one of those nights on call when you leave at 7am thinking you'll be back home by 6pm turns into a back at 3am in the morning trip, had not fared so well. They had begun to melt into a puddle of chocolate and peanuts all wrapped up in a yellow bag. Not to worry, they would solidify again as the summer turned to fall and then winter. They would certainly be available for that late night pick-me up later in the year.

My next patient was Mrs. Compact, a 95 year-old sweetheart brought into the office by her young, 75 year-old daughter. It seems that the nursing home had failed to monitor Mrs. Compact's bowel protocol and it had now been over a week since she had defecated. And, thus, the pseudonym compact(ed) would apply. This is not a good thing, as you can imagine. My blessed nurse and I now had the job of relieving all the pain we could by evacuating the bowel. Yes, this is done the old fashioned way, using a gloved hand and reaching up the rectum, as far as you can, to "spoon" out whatever you can get your fingers around.

It is as horrible a job as you are certainly imagining. This really stinks. But who said the practice of medicine was all glamour and no glory? Did I say glory?

We set out on our mission with lots of enthusiasm, knowing our efforts would not only relieve this sweet lady of immense pain, but there were certainly eternal rewards ahead for us, as well. There *must* be for completing a job this nasty. Anyway, two gloves, lots of pushing, shoving, moaning, and screaming, (by the patient that is), we were making progress. This was measured in tonnage, by the way. In addition, there is no way to use that room again for at least a day and a half. But, having done a job well and retreating to my office to let my nurse complete the final cleaning process, a sinister thought came to my mind. What about those chocolate covered peanuts that had been deteriorating in my pick up truck? I quickly raced to get them. I then covered my mouth with melted chocolate as if I had been eating my first chocolate after being incarcerated for 20 years. My nurse fell right into my trap. She walked into my office and said, "That was the worst thing I have ever had to do." I turned in my swivel chair to face her and said, "Hey, do you want some chocolate?" She nearly puked!

More Then Meets the Eye

"For every problem in the world there is a simple, obvious, wrong answer." I was told that once and sometimes, I still believe it. Yet, experience has taught me that still, many times, there *are* much simpler solutions to the problems that people in management seem to be trying to solve. Unfortunately, wisdom and experience are not required assets for most managerial positions. The same principles should apply to your physician's office practice. It would seem that the process of making an appointment, checking the patient in, providing the necessary medical services, and calling in the medicine to the pharmacy would be a simple, well-honed practice. This couldn't be further from the truth. This is why we call it the *practice* of medicine. There is nothing like throwing an actual patient into the milieu to really mess things up.

I was called once about a patient who showed up at the emergency room after having fallen off his bicycle. I was asked if I would see him in follow up as he had been assigned to me. This seems simple enough except I had never met this patient before. He had apparently been transferred to my care after the third-year residents had graduated and left their clinic patients to those of us just beginning our residency training. This patient had been on coumadin, a blood thinner. He hadn't had his blood level checked for a couple of months because some managerial genius had decided to close the laboratory during the lunch hour to save time and money. Unfortunately, due to his college course schedule, the lunch hour was the only time this patient could come into the clinic. He now had an INR of 17. We usually like it to be 2. That means that his blood was about *17 times* thinner than yours or mine. We can only be glad that he hadn't cut himself shaving.

He was eventually scheduled to see me in the office and was put in for a "brief office visit." This is meant to last from 5 to 10 minutes. How long should it take to recheck somebody's blood level on coumadin therapy anyway? Now, meet Mr. Tinker.

"Why are you on coumadin anyway?" I asked.

"I had a pulmonary embolism," he responded.

"Wow, that's unusual in such a young, active man," I replied.

"Well, it happened after my leg was crushed,"

"How did *that* happen?" I quizzed him.

"It happened after the truck ran over my leg," he retorted.

"How did *that* happen?" I dug deeper.

"Well, I tried to commit suicide," he startled me.

"Why would you do something like that?" I offered.

"I was suffering from severe depression," he informed me.

"Why should a nice, young man like you be depressed?" I psychoanalyzed.

"My father and mother sexually abused me when I was young," he said in remorse.

"Would you like to talk about that?" I empathized.

"Well, it all started back when I was four years old," he began.

And I thought this was going to be a brief office visit. We have been good friends ever sense and I still run behind in my office schedule almost every time he is in the clinic.

Welcome to Scheduling 101.

Excuse Me for Going to Medical School

One thing that drives a physician nuts, is the intrusion of others into his or her medical practice. It's bad enough when a *teacher* can get credit for marketing a vitamin supplement as a medicine (oooooohhh). It's even worse when it's the United States government.

I have often had to do battle with a school nurse over whether children are properly immunized. The child comes in at 3 years, eleven months and fifteen days of age to get an immunization for Measles, Mumps and Rubella (MMR). We give it at this age because it's around this time that children are at the greatest risk for these diseases. Otherwise, we are unlikely to see the child again until they're seventeen and getting a pregnancy test. But what do we hear from the school nurse? "They are supposed to get their MMR at 4 years of age." **BIG DEAL**. Do you really think their body cares whether the immunization is given 15 days earlier than your little piece of paper says it should? **NO IT DOESN'T**.

Even worse than the school nurse, is an event that happened to me just a week ago. A young man had shaved for the very first time and ended up getting an impetiginous infection around his face. No big deal. But it was certainly important enough to treat him with an antibiotic which I did both topically as well as orally.

Before the day was over, I had received two phone calls. The first was from the infamous school nurse saying that I should do a culture to rule out MRSA (Methacillin resistant Staphylococcus aureus). I informed her that the lesions were not purulent (pus producing) and therefore a culture was not necessarily indicated. In fact, getting a culture would be harmful and oh, by the way, TRAUMATIC. Remember the "first do no harm" section of the Hippocratic Oath. I also figured that I would see the patient back in a day or two if things weren't getting better. The kid's mom and dad weren't idiots.

Never to let it die, I later received another phone call from the principle who said that he thought that the kid should be treated for Herpes gladiatorum. He insisted that we see the kid again to reconsider. The principle had herpes when he was in high school 25 years ago and that is what it looked like to him. "Herpes," by the way, means "grouped" and these lesions certainly were not.

I saw the patient again the next day under duress from the school and he was already getting much better. I guess my ability to diagnose and treat was still intact. But what can a Board Certified physician say to a school nurse and her over-zealous principle? Excuse me for going to medical school and trying to practice medicine without your governmental oversight. I told the parents to send the second bill to the school district.

Ode to Marty Feldman

Have you ever had one of those times when you just couldn't keep your mouth shut? Maybe it was in rebuttal to a comment someone else has said that conflicts with your religious or political views. For me, it occasionally happens when I realize that I could really help someone out who, unfortunately has not asked me for medical advice. This is rare, by the way, as we physicians usually get asked medical advice *all the time*. And I don't mean when we are in the office. I don't believe it happens in many other professions, but I could be wrong. I suppose a sex therapist could be another example, but short of that, I assume we stand fairly alone. I even had a woman stand up in an airplane once and show me a mole she was concerned about on her lower thigh—I kid you not—after I made the mistake of revealing my professional status. And, by the way, she wasn't hot enough for me to enjoy it.

Occasionally, I will see a kid at the store or in church with acne and know that with a simple antibiotic at about $6-a-month, they could have a much better complexion and eventually, much more self-confidence. Another example would be the story of Marty.

Marty came to see me for a pre-college physical. This would include a simple, basic sports physical exam and a review and update of her immunizations. However, what was immediately obvious was her thyroid problem and the signs and symptoms of Grave's disease. In Grave's disease, the thyroid gland over-produces and raises the thyroxin level. The muscles that control eye movements hypertrophy and begin to cause the eyes to "bug out." Marty Feldman remains the prime example. This Marty had it badly. In fact, she was practically pushing her glasses off her face. No, I mean it!

The problem was, no matter what question I used to query whether she was aware of her medical condition, I received a null response.

"Have you had any past medical problems?"

"None, she responded."

"Are you taking any medicine?"

"No."

"Is there a family history of medical issues with mom or dad?"

"None that I know of," she answered clearly.

"Have you seen any other physicians before?"

"Not really."

Finally, after dragging the physical out as long as I could in order to get up the nerve to address her biggest problem, she mentioned that she was having surgery that summer when school would be out.

"What are you having surgery for?" I asked.

"To put these eyeballs back into my skull."

Boy was I relieved.

Happy Father's Day

Heroin addiction is a very sad thing. A person's life starts out joyfully as they are brought into the world, usually full of hope and with great expectations. And then, life happens. The very nature of man itself raises its ugly head and tragic environmental circumstances push some individuals to a life less hopeful than initially planned.

As a third year resident in medicine, I was allowed by law to "moonlight," an opportunity we take to earn a little money before we actually complete residency itself. We are already doctors with some training so we usually moonlight in order to start paying back those medical school loans we are all famous for owing. I made about $30,000 my last year of training, which turns out to be about $3.42 an hour. Believe me, with a wife and three children, supplementing my income helped.

My moonlighting experience entailed an opportunity to do methadone physicals in a program that was specifically designed to help heroin addicts enter treatment facilities and hopefully start a new life again. Methadone is a drug used to wean an addict off heroin because it has a much longer "half-life" and dissipates from the body much more slowly. Methadone also helps control withdrawal symptoms as it is tapered away. Great in theory, but unfortunately, it often falls far short in reality. My high school physical education teacher summed it up in one word, "Yougottawanna."

One of the physicals I most remember completing was that of a young 28 year-old woman who had the right attitude and, I suppose for her, the methadone treatment may have been successful. She had first found hope through a religious organization, and with the help of loving friends, had come to start her new life. Unfortunately, I couldn't care less that morning. Another drug physical, another fifty bucks was the attitude I had developed. Pathetic!

I ran through all the requirements to complete the physical exam and the necessary paperwork, caring little about her story initially. Interestingly however, I did notice that she had apparently had bilateral knee replacements. She had eight-inch, longitudinal scars down the anterior aspect of each knee. This was certainly unusual for a person her age. Naively, I asked her if she was a skier or had she had an accident that may have damaged her knees so badly that she needed them replaced so early in life.

I was shocked back into reality when she told me, "No, that's what happens when your father breaks your knees with a baseball bat." Happy Father's day?! In her shoes, any of us could easily have found ourselves hooked on heroin.

My father was deceased at that time, but I said a prayer to the *Heavenly* Father that day, thanking Him for the loving father He had given to me.

Family Medicine

There is a common misunderstanding with the term family medicine. This term apparently entitles everyone even remotely related to the physician to be treated free of charge and at any time of the day. This includes the immediate family and even someone who your mom says you *might* be related to, like King Richard the Lion Heart. It also crosses all state and national boundaries. This term includes free medical advice and information encompassing the entire scope of the medical dictionary, as well as the free prescribing and distribution of any and all medicine for these recommendations. Had I known this when I was choosing my specialty at the end of medical school, I would have chosen proctology. Now I doubt that *they* are ever called out in the middle of the night.

Don't get me wrong. I love a few of the people in my family that at least carry the same sir name. These would be my wife and three children. I would also extend that sphere of concern to many other family and friends who I at least see on a regular basis in my life and even the above mentioned persons' friends. "Your friends are my friends," as they say. It is those *extended* family members and *their* friends that test my inclination not to perform the two-fingered, digital-rectal exam when they only have a cold. This exam is usually performed with one finger by the way. No twisting allowed. And you are supposed to remove all your rings.

I think it is actually the lack of appreciation for the services rendered that causes me to vent here. You know, like not even saying hello when they eventually come to your house for family gatherings. Only when the party begins to die down a little do they finally acknowledge you and then only to ask, "Can you just look at little Bobbie for a possible ear infection?" "I did see him pull at his ear yesterday in the car." I am sure it couldn't be his long hair tickling his ear because he should have had a hair cut about two months ago. "And he did have a fever yesterday measured at 99.1 (normal temperature averages 98.6) but his always runs a little lower so 98.7 is really a fever of 104 degrees."

The worst of it all is that I have even had to discharge a couple of family members from my actual office practice because they never paid their bill to my office staff. Yes, I employ a few staff members that really don't want to give up their salaries just so the Doctor's extended family and friends can get their medical care free. By the way, this was a natural process from the billing department that I had no control over. Yes, this causes a few rifts in the family tree but "Business is business and business must grow," as the Lorax once said.

Don't think that I am being too horrible. I didn't go into medicine for the money. But this is something that bothers everyone in the profession. Yes, even *your* brother or sister or mother or father or aunt or uncle or distant relative that has a degree in medicine but "really doesn't mind treating you since you are so close"-like 4 states away.

My kids have really picked up the ball on this too. You see, my being called out effects them too. This is now time away from their dad. They have learned to answer the phone for me and screen the calls better than the staff I mentioned earlier. My staff says, "It's your cousin on line one. No, it's just a friendly call and not a medical question." The friendly part lasts just a few seconds before the real call starts. I usually hear a very brief "hello-how-has-your-mother-been-doing-lately," before I begin to hear about their nephew's-pregnant-girlfriend-whose-doctor-doesn't-know-anything-and-told-her-that-nausea-is-normal-in-pregnancy story. I only take a second to remind them that my mother has been dead for five years, but they should already know this since we are *so close*. My children do much better screening these calls. They hold the phone away from their mouth just far enough that eardrums don't break on the line of origination and shout across the room to me, "Hey Dad, I didn't think that you were on call again *this* week!" Silly kids, don't even know my own call schedule. But after all, I did go into family medicine, didn't I?

Hare Lip

One of the reasons I went to medical school in the first place was to be able to deliver babies. Yet, one of the best things that happened in my medical career was to stop delivering babies. The process of giving birth is a truly remarkable process. Just studying the process from conception to the actual birth of a human life is nearly sensual. How someone can learn the steps in this miracle and still not believe in a Divine Creator is beyond me. It must be truly a spiritual issue, as it surely can't be one of mere intelligence.

Now the delivery of babies comes in two flavors. One flavor is very sweet, indeed. It results when a confident mother easily follows the prescribed directions outlined by the Master and pushes out a new wonderful life and the physician is able to be back at home either in bed or reading a book in about an hour. This rarely happens, by the way. When it does, the physician will often be unable to believe that they even get paid for doing this profession. It is truly a wonderful thing.

The other flavor is far more—bitter. It is usually someone who forgot to read the manual on easy deliveries and ends up taking either several hours to finish the process or makes every step not only unforgettable but also miserable. I mean for all the rest of us involved. It can be the most horrifying, alert your lawyer provoking, grey hair changing experience in the world. At these times, the physician realizes that they aren't being paid enough. Realistically, most deliveries land somewhere in-between. Fortunately, the physician usually has very little to contribute to either flavor. Women have been delivering babies for centuries without medical help and I suggest they continue to limit the interference of the medical profession as much as possible.

I remember many of the deliveries I had the fortune of helping along. One stands out especially to me because it involved the delivery of a baby with the misfortune of having a cleft lip and palate. After noticing this unfortunate circumstance, I carefully concealed the baby from the mother by whisking the newborn over to the nursing attendants as I began to choose my words very carefully. I needed to break the news professionally and in as comforting a manner as possible to help the mother receive this possibly devastating news as reassuringly as possible. With other members of her family present, I very carefully explained that sometimes things go wrong in the formation of the baby which sometimes results in birth defects. I explained that some of these can be repaired with surgery after the baby begins to grow and becomes stronger. I then explained that just such a thing had happened to her special baby girl and that she had been born with what we refer to as a cleft lip and palate.

She accepted this news seemingly well and with great stoicism. I was trying to be as close to the mother as I possibly could in this intimate moment between physician and patient. When her family asked what I was saying, she blurted out, "He said the baby has a hare lip." I most certainly did not. So much for professional candor.

I Never Forget a Rectum, Butt in Your Case, I'll Make an Exception.

Few things in life provoke as much fear, or at least as much trepidation, as a colonoscopy. Even the shortened version of sliding up the "Hershey Highway," a flexible sigmoidoscopy, is dreaded by most. (Well, at least for the one on the *receiving* end, and not necessarily for the physician.) And yet, a few of these actually have provoked a great deal of humor. (Well, at least for the *physician* and not necessarily the one on the receiving end.) I'll actually never forget the first flexible sigmoidoscopy I ever performed. It has kept me laughing as I go through the years of practicing medicine.

The first sigmoidoscopy I performed was on a poor older man who needed one for screening purposes. I say poor, not because he didn't have any money, but only because he was the guinea pig for my first attempt in the maze. We'll call him Bob for privacy sake. He had reported no rectal bleeding and no defecation problems. But we wanted to eliminate the likelihood of having a hidden, growing tumor just waiting to pounce upon him in the later years of his life. As this made the whole process less critical, I was offered the opportunity to test my maneuverability skills as a first year resident in Family Medicine.

How this procedure is *supposed* to work is this: First, you prepare yourself by cleansing the bowel a day or so before by drinking, or rather choking down, a gallon of "Go Lytely." This stuff alone has to be provoking a great deal of laughter in the guy who first invented and then named this solution. You don't "go lightly" at all. In fact, it completely evacuates the bowel over the next 24 hours. Forget about leaving the house or going to work unless you deliver port-a-potties for a living. Rather, he should have named it "Blast Off" or "Dynamite" or something similar. Regardless, it is designed to empty your bowel so that the physician can not only maneuver his way through the colon visually unimpaired, but also so that he can discern whether there are any bad things growing. Sounds simple, doesn't it?

How we can put a man on the moon and bring him back again but are unable to create a pill that will clean out the colon in a half-an-hour, perplexes me. I came up with the thought of using a Rotavirus once but nobody has picked up on that idea to bring it to fruition. This is the virus that causes the greater percentage of viral gastroenteritis cases anyway and it usually does the same job of clearing the bowel completely as all of us have probably experienced at one time or another. Anyway, once the prep has been completed, it is then time for the procedure itself. I recommend not using a first year medicine resident, by the way. I'm sure Bob would agree.

Second, you undergo "a simple office procedure." The physician "maneuvers" or "shoves" a 4 to 6 foot tube up your rectum that is wired for lights and camera. It is also designed to turn corners, moving up or down and left or right, all by use of one hand. It is quite slick actually. We look for polyps and diverticuli that may be hiding there and increasing the risk for troubles in the future.

Unfortunately, there is a caveat. The rectum and bowel are usually closed. To maneuver the scope, you need to first inflate the bowel with air. This is easy to do as the scope is also equipped with an air source, a pump, and suction. Another caveat, the bowel only feels pain with inflation, not with actual cutting. This is convenient for taking biopsies but makes inflation of the bowel to just the right diameter the key trick to overcome. If the bowel gets hyper-inflated, the patient writhes in pain. We all have felt this when we have the pressure mounting before a bowel movement and there is no bathroom in sight.

As a first year resident, and perhaps not the best one, I was especially eager to inflate the bowel and start the maneuvering. Unfortunately for Bob, I hadn't been told about caveat number two yet. After the writhing subsided, secondary to him passing out, the attending physician (name withheld for the safety of the physician) had me stop and reassess. Of course, by this time, I had inflated enough air to practically lift Bob off the table. He actually would have if I had used helium or his anal sphincter hadn't given out and allowed him to pass enough air out into the room equal to the dose I was pushing in. Somehow this must be related to Boyle's ideal gas law. This may have actually saved his life but it was sure stinking up the exam room.

I remember the attending physician saying, "We have learned two important things today. One is why I only use as little air as possible and the other is why I always wear a mask." By the way, if I ever have to have a sigmoid or colonoscopy, I want the physician to use laughing gas. Sorry Bob.

It's a Small World After All!

It's a small world after all! Disney has made a fortune off that phrase. And although I have never been to one of their amusement parks, I understand that they have a whole section dedicated to just that theme. And it really is true. It *is* a small world after all. Nearly everyone has experienced traveling somewhere that have never been only to meet someone from our own backyard or someone who knows someone that they know, etc…

One such experience that sticks out in my mind was when I traveled to the jungles of Guatemala. As a third year resident in medicine and as a Christian physician, I was invited to join a team of medical, dental, optometric, and spiritual staff to go on a medical mission to a known vacation spot. NOT! The team was made up of about twenty medical professionals and support staff. We were to go deep into the jungle to bring supplies and provide medical, dental, and optometric services to those much less fortunate than us. That's right, the *jungle*. You know, "Lions and tigers and bears, Oh my!" "Lions and tigers and bears, Oh my!" Except, it was more like "Spiders and snakes and whoknowswhat, Oh my!" "Spiders and snakes and whoknowswhat, Oh my!" You get the picture.

So one nice autumn morning, after months of planning, we loaded up a few trucks of supplies and began a two week journey to go "where no man had gone before." Well, at least none of *us* had ever been there. We left Yakima, Washington and began a forty-eight hour trip that started by truck and ended on foot to the jungles of Guatemala. After an initial drive to Seattle, Washington, we boarded a plane that flew us through LAX (speaking of a jungle) and then directly to Guatemala City. And that was only the beginning. Did I mention that there are really no roads in Guatemala?

Once we landed, the journey *really* began. We have all seen the movies that show the bus load of passengers mixed with chickens and produce, as a well as, suspect characters who ramble on through mud and mire escaping tragedy after tragedy but only by the skin of their teeth. We literally lived that scene. Travel on the Guatemalan roads actually took more time than if you had decided to go on foot. But foot traffic wouldn't have let you experience the sensation of motion sickness and nausea from diesel-fumes all at once. Needless to say, it was a long road trip.

However, by the grace of God and His providential hand, we arrived at our destination unscathed. Except for a few bowel troubles and perhaps a few tired bones, we trudged our last few miles through the jungle to our predetermined destination.

And what is the first thing I see after forty-eight hours of said travel? There was a Guatemalan native wearing a hat that said, *Akland Irrigation-* Yakima, Washington. This was the very same small company I used for my own irrigation needs back home. It truly is a small world after all.

Just a Poor Boy
Who Went to College

Most people still have a healthy respect for the medical profession. That's good. Most of the physicians that are out there caring for their patients deserve that respect. And most people believe that those physicians got to their position because they are exceptionally smart. That can't be further from the truth. Yes, it does take a certain level of intelligence to survive the application process. And yes, it also may take some intelligence to survive the rigors of 30-36 credit hours per semester, the actual workload of the training itself. (To put that in perspective, most college students take from 15-18 credits per quarter or semester; so you can image what doubling that work load would mean.) But most of us are just driven people and not exceptionally smart. And the only thing that gets us through medical school is an insatiable desire to study the greatest subject in the world: the construction, design and the physiology of the human body. It is truly unbelievable. The Psalmist says it best in Psalms 139:14 ... "I am fearfully and wonderfully made." We are also driven by the fact that we are going in debt at a tremendous speed and we will need to be a doctor to ever pay our way out of it.

All that being said, it is easy for doctors to get an ego that makes them think they are better than everyone else. This is sad, but true. As for me, I remember a seasoned old physician giving me some words of wisdom as I went off to medical school, "Don't forget, you are just a country boy that got to go to college."

Little did I know how that would affect me. I was just finishing one of the most taxing areas of my medical school training. I was completing an emergency medicine clerkship at Harborview Medical Center in Seattle, Washington. Harborview can be best pictured as a scene right out of *ER,* the television series. I would literally see people arrive with butcher knives sticking out of their chest or gun shot wounds leaving gaping holes where parts of their body had just been. And even as a student, I would literally stitch people's wounds closed for 12 hours straight during my shift.

It is also during this part of our training where we learn ALS (Advanced Life Support). We learn to use the medicines and paddles that shock people back to life when they try dying on us. You try to keep this from happening on *your* shift. The end of the training is concluded by a rigorous paper and oral examination. And a miracle occurred that day. I finished with the highest grade in my class.

I was naturally feeling more than a little proud of that accomplishment when I now reported for my last shift to complete the rotation. I had worked and studied hard and the dividends had paid off. And admittedly, I was feeling pretty arrogant. Then the Lord finished His work.

The first patient I was asked to care for was a chronic alcoholic who had a blood alcohol level of over .600. (Legal limit in my state of Washington is .08) That is *seven times* the legal limit. Few people can handle that without dying. If they do die it's because we say, "he had a little too much blood in their alcohol stream." This guy was so pickled, I didn't even need to use anesthesia to close his wounds, although I did.

The worst part was how much he smelled. He was covered in feces and vomit and I had to clean him up to even find where he was bleeding. How had I gone from the highest grade in the class to scrubbing the feet of a drunk? As he cussed and spit on me while I scrubbed his feet and began the stitching process, I felt a humbling spirit descend upon me. I truly believe it was the Holy Spirit reminding me of the saying of that wise old physician, "Don't forget, you're just a country boy that got to go to college." Thank you Lord, and pass the smelling salts.

Referrals

Many of you that frequent a physician only once or twice in your lifetime may not even know what a referral is. For those that visit more often, referrals may be the bane of your medical life. Do you want to visit a Cardiologist to have your heart examined? You most likely will need a referral. Do you need a colonoscopy to fulfill that request from your wife as you hit the magical age of fifty? You may need that referral again.

Referrals are often required by insurance companies and government controlled medial groups, such as state sponsored Medicaid or nationally sponsored Medicare, to actually help keep the costs of medicine down. That may not make sense immediately as you can already calculate the fact that two office visits should be more expensive than one. But that may not actually be the case. The specialists usually charge more than those that practice general medicine, such as your Internal Medicine Physician, Pediatrician, or Family Physician. They go to residency training another year or two which somehow apparently merits the charge difference.

The overall thought from the insurance side is that there are many things a generalist can do and many times a specialist isn't even needed. Also, many times, if the problem is capable of being handled by a generalist, the specialist may not even want to see you. They would rather be doing the more exotic cases that justified the extra training we spoke of earlier. Unfortunately, often times the patient doesn't know the difference. Do you have high blood pressure? We generalists can usually handle that. Do you have acne? We can handle that too. Constipation, chest pain, headaches, blurred vision? You guessed it, we can handle that as well.

Another misconception is that the generalists stopped their training early and the specialists did everything we did and then continued on for more. This couldn't be further from the truth. An Anesthesiologist, for example, couldn't help you with your urinary tract infection, sinusitis, pneumonia, or hemorrhoids any more than your auto mechanic. They typically don't know how to make these diagnoses, how to differentiate them from more serious problems, or even what medicines are usually prescribed. They are great at what they do but they are not meant to be on the front line, which presents a need for the referral. As a Family Physician, let me take a look, and then I'll refer you if necessary.

One referral I made recently was for a woman who had onychomycosis. She had developed a fungal infection in many of her toenails which caused them to be very thick, unsightly, and painful whenever she tried to wear shoes. Unfortunately for her, she was quite elderly and I worried about prescribing medicines that may do the job of curing her unsightly toes but would also take a few months and may actually damage her liver. She asked me if I could refer her to a specialist such as a Podiatrist. After accessing how thick those toenails actually were, I told her "No, but I know a good blacksmith."

See One, Do One, Teach One

Your physician has spent a long time getting his education. Make no doubt about it. After graduating from high school, the usual pattern is to first obtain a Bachelor of Science degree in a field of science. This takes four years, unless you are Doogie Hauser, who really doesn't exist. Even if he wasn't a fictional character, I sure wouldn't want him taking care of me because medicine isn't just about being smart. The practice of medicine is about caring. How many teenagers are there in the world that care for anyone other than themselves? The obvious answer is NONE. I have three great children who are all adults now and gave my wife and I absolutely no rebellious signs growing up. *Really.* And yet they all admit that they only thought of themselves through those teenage years.

My bachelor's degree was in Bacteriology. I thought the name sounded great so I started taking classes in the subject and, before I knew it, it was too late to change majors again. So there I was, stuck looking at bacteria under a microscope. At least I *think* those were bacteria. They could have been specks of dirt on the glass slide, for all I knew. Anyway, they gave me a degree so at least I graduated. Then it was on to medical school for another four years. Of course, you have to apply for these positions which are few in number and highly competitive.

How I got in is still a miracle—dwarfing even Moses and the Israelites crossing the Red Sea in their flight out of Egypt (see Exodus 14).

What they never told me about medical school was that now I had to take 30-36 credits a quarter rather than the 15-17 credits I took in undergrad. Who thought of that system? At least in undergrad I had time to go to the bathroom and eat lunch. Now I had to do both at the same time. And you have to learn to watch this step very carefully or you die.

Four years and 49,082 hours later, it is off to residency. You do the math. This is where you begin learning the specialty of choice that you will practice for the rest of your medical career. The examples most familiar to the average lay person are Internal Medicine, Pediatrics, General Surgery, Family Medicine, and Orthopedic Surgery. Each of these takes no less than three years, but at least you are getting paid—unfortunately at about $2.93 per hour. But at the end they call you Doctor and somehow that makes those 11 years all seem worth it. "Can I get you something, Doctor?" "What do you think, Doctor?" It does feel rather good.

The point of the story is that even though you have 11 or more years under your belt, you know almost nothing. The breadth of medicine is so vast that you have usually only seen many things once. Thus, with procedures, say a craniotomy, you have usually seen someone do it. Then you had to do it yourself once and now you are qualified to teach the younger physician standing behind you at the operating table. Thus, "see one, do one, teach one." What a system for building confidence huh? That is really how it goes, although I may be stretching the craniotomy part a bit. Since the brain is involved, you actually see two of these before you get to do one.

And now, let the cover up begin. "Have you ever done this before?" You ask your doctor. "I have never had a problem with this procedure before," he retorts back. That means they have probably done only one, maybe not. "I have never, ever had a problem with this procedure before." That means they have done two. "In my series of these, I have never had a problem with this procedure before." They have done three. You get the picture.

The only thing worse than this is when you are already out in practice and are doing it blind for the first time. I had a patient walk in after falling and dislocating his shoulder. Well, that's the conclusion I came to because he came in splinting his arm and said, "I think I have dislocated my shoulder." After a quick series of x-rays to buy enough time for me to look up in a book how to reduce it, I asked my partners if they had ever reduced a shoulder separation before. I received a universal, "Nope." We had *seen* it before but had never actually done it ourselves.

After consultation with the latest throw away medical manual, we decided to do the Thompson method, only because that's the one they mentioned first. The x-ray technician was too good and didn't give us time to study the other methods. With the Thompson method, you pull down on the hanging arm while the patient lays face down on the exam table. We gave him something to relax him of course. We weren't Doogy Hauser. I then applied the "downward steady pressure" as described in the manual. After about 11 minutes (I'm really good apparently because the book said 17-20 minutes), I felt a pop. The patient felt immediately healed and I was a miracle worker, once more. I sent him for an MRI to verify he hadn't broken his labrum and all was well. He was back swinging an axe before he had time to ask, "Have you ever done this before, Doctor?"

Rights and Privileges

When I graduated from medical school and was given my diploma that verified completion of all the requirements to anyone who cared, I remember them saying that this came "with all the rights and privileges" of being a physician. Now, I am not sure what rights and privileges they were referring to but I assume those should be coming any day now. Perhaps they should have just said "with all the obligations and responsibilities." Now to those, I can testify.

One of the responsibilities that comes with that medical diploma is the need to share news with patients. Sometimes that news is good and sometimes that news is bad. Unfortunately, you don't get to choose. How do you tell someone that they have cancer or that their precious baby has been born with a devastating birth defect? There is no easy way, so I never pretend that there is. I give that information straightforward and honestly. I try to show as much compassion as possible and always try to put myself in their shoes. I usually tell them that they are in a battle but I am going to do my best to help them win the war.

Fortunately, most of the time, the news is good. Most biopsies are *negative* which is good in medicine. For example, a biopsy is *negative* for cancer or test results are *negative* for abnormal findings. You get the drift. But even giving this news can be a challenge. The patient has been waiting a few days for the results and there is a lot of anxiety that has built up. I usually try to use a little humor to break the ice.

I often come in and say, "I have some good news." They of course smile as the relief dissipates from their face. I then tell them, "I just saved $300.00 by switching to Geico." This may sound cheesy but it always creates a lot of laughter. I quickly tell them that their test results are good too. We then share the good news of their lab, biopsy, or test results. We also share in the humor of me trying to bring a little levity to "all those rights and privileges." Of course, I don't attempt humor if those results are bad. Otherwise, I may be looking for another type of insurance besides Geico, called malpractice.

I Saved Her Life You Know

In the everyday experience of being a Family Medicine Physician, curing those who needed to see you before they got better all by themselves, there is occasionally a reason for celebration. It is those events that keep the physician at the grind stone, so-to-speak, and occasionally, makes stories that are worth remembering.

One such occasion occurred early in my medical career. In fact, I was still in my medical residency (year 11 of my training). I was asked to come and see a patient that was new to me and practically any other physician. Although she was an 80 year-old, care worn woman who reminded me of Auntie Em from the Wizard of Oz, she rarely needed a physician's help. She had probably had a mild heart attack a few days before and had now slipped into congestive heart failure. Unable to accommodate her fluid overload from all her daily salt consumption, she began to swell. It started in her legs and then backed up into the lungs. This gave her such shortness of breath that it prompted a visit to the emergency room which is where I met her.

The nice thing about mild congestive heart failure is that it is usually treatable with a "little water pill." Physicians call it Lasix although the real name is furosimide (don't worry about pronunciation). The key to Lasix is that it makes you pee like a race horse for about six (**la**sts **six)** hours. It is designed to get rid of all that fluid you have been accumulating. You can imagine what that does for the breathing problem. It allows them to breathe and exchange oxygen once again. The patient usually feels much better in just a short period of time.

To Beulah, it felt as though I had saved her life. And she told everybody she met that I had done just that—for the next ten years. And I mean *everybody*.

Approximately five years after the congestive heart failure incident, I was called to admit her for a broken hip. As the nurse called to give me the details of her fall and subsequent orthopedic problem, I jokingly told her that I had saved Beulah's life once. "Oh, we know." She had already told them all about it. It's great to be a hero once in a while.

9-11

It was just a month or so after 9-11 (September 11, 2001)-a day that shall live in infamy, as President Roosevelt would have said as he did after the Japanese attack on Pearl Harbor in 1941. The Twin Towers of New York City had just fallen and to many of us, every Muslim was now a jihadist just waiting for his or her opportunity to destroy America.

I was on the island of Hawaii participating in an orthopedic CME (Continuing Medical Education). As physicians, we are required to have fifty hours of new education per year in order to retain our medical license. My wife and I had flown to Kona to not only partake in the CME but to also soak in some long-awaited sunshine. Part of the CME also provided an opportunity for us to work as medical staff at the Iron man triathlon. Every year, hundreds of the world's greatest athletes swim 2.4 miles, bicycle 112 miles, and finish by running a 26.3-mile marathon. We were there to assist them in finishing that great test of athleticism.

As a physician, I was given a special shirt to wear that easily identified me as a team doctor. It provided me easy access to many of the venues. If there was a closed gate being monitored by special staff, I got right in. If there were supplies guarded by another staff member, I got them easily. It wasn't a fancy shirt, but it provided the access I needed.

I had just finished helping at the second stage of the triathlon, where participants transitioned from the bicycle race to the marathon. Armed guards protected their $10,000 to $20,000 bicycles while I assessed whether each athlete had any personal needs as they donned running shoes and shorts to start the marathon. Then I walked the mile or two back to the start of the race, where each would finish the race sometime before midnight.

It was along this coastal route that I was confronted by what I would describe as a Middle-Eastern male of about twenty years of age. He asked me where I got my shirt and if he could buy one. I told him that it was special and joked that he could buy it from me for $400. I was startled when he took out his wallet and prepared to do just that.

Recognizing that this could be serious, and being paranoid that everyone that looked like him was out to destroy America, I laughed and said that I was just kidding. I walked away with mixed emotions. Had I just been confronted by a jihadist who wanted my shirt to gain access to places he shouldn't be? And hey, maybe I should have asked for $800?

It Cuts Both Ways

Yes, this is the day for being politically correct. Not for me, so much, but it seems so for many of the self-righteous world. One area of special sensitivity seems to lie in the world of sports, specifically in determining the name of your team and choosing the mascot. When I grew up, we all looked forward to the big game between the Cowboys and the Redskins. We all knew what that meant and no one minded, not even the Redskins, I mean the Native Americans. How would I know? I grew up with them. In fact, I was surrounded by probably the most diverse, multicultural neighborhood in the world. We had us Honkies (Caucasians, which would include those of Dutch, Italian, British and French descent) living and playing right next to the Indians (Native-Americans), the Spics (Hispanics), the Flips (Filipinos), a few blacks (African-Americans) and even a community of Japs (Japanese). Sometimes we argued, sometimes we fought, but most of the time we just loved on each other and loved on each other a lot.

Enter the new age of hypersensitivity. This is where people assume a god-like, self-evaluating, and often condescending heir about themselves. Now, all of a sudden, everyone seems more enlightened about their ancestry and we all have to walk on egg shells lest we offend a WASP (White Anglo Saxon Protestant) as my Chink (Chinese) boss once called me. What does my Caucasian race and religious preference have to do with anything? "Make them quit hurting my feelings!"

I recently encountered a funny incident related to this while practicing the art of medicine. A young, seven year-old boy was brought into the office to have some cryotherapy applied to a few Verrucus vulgaris spots (common warts). This is where we apply a little liquid nitrogen to freeze the wart and help rid the body of these unsightly things that grow on the body. As anyone knows who has had it done, this hurts a little. This young boy knew that and he started to cry.

I was especially surprised to hear the comforting words of his eighty year-old grandmother as she hugged and consoled him through the procedure. She placed her care worn arms around him and said, "Just Cowboy up." I had to laugh. He was an Indian.—I mean, a Native American.

Keep the Change

I had just seen 4 year-old Maddie about a week before when Mom brought her into the office for her routine well-child check. A well-child check is a special examination that we physicians perform at periodic times to assure both the parents and the physician that the child is growing and developing physically, mentally, and socially. Maddie had done just fine on her check up, so I was surprised to see her back in my office so soon.

Maddie has an intelligent mother who works as a flight nurse. She said that she brought Maddie back into the clinic because she had forgotten to tell me that Maddie hadn't been eating very well over the past couple of weeks. She had no fevers, no vomiting, and no diarrhea. Her activity level had been unchanged, as well. But every time she started to eat a meal, Maddie would choke a little and stop.

I reexamined Maddie, as I had done a week or so earlier, and again, nothing seemed wrong. Her vital signs were normal. Her throat and neck were without any abnormalities. Her stomach was soft and non-tender. I reassured mom that every thing seemed just fine and that we could just watch her a few more days. Then there was the rest of the story.

Mom said that perhaps she should mention that she had caught Maddie playing with her coin purse about two weeks prior. However, other than a scolding or two, she seemed just fine after that.

I ordered an immediate chest x-ray, of course. I was sure a coin would be found somewhere in the esophagus. But I was wrong. It was completely clear. However, I had wished that the x-ray had been taken just a teeny weenie bit of an inch higher so that it might include more of the throat area. This is fairly easy to do on a young child where body size is small. I explained to mom that the likelihood of finding something was minimal and I wanted to limit radiation exposure. But perhaps we should retake the x-ray just one more time. Fortunately, she agreed.

There it was on the retake. A shiny quarter was lodged vertically in the superior esophagus. Every time Maddie attempted to eat, the quarter apparently turned sideways and blocked her ability to swallow. We didn't have the tools to take it out safely, although I admit, I was tempted to just turn her upside down and shake, not stir (of course). But if it dislodged and then went into her trachea, she could be in even bigger trouble. So, off she went with her mother in a helicopter to the nearest Pediatric Gastroenterologist a few hours away. Mom and I still laugh after each office visit now when I tell Maddie, "And keep the change."

Open Mouth, Insert Foot

As a physician, I believe that pharmaceutical representatives can be of great help in the doctor's office. In addition to providing educational materials for the patients and physicians, they often provide patients with sample medicines free of charge. This allows me to try new medicines, gage their affectivity, and test their side effect profiles without making the patient bear the burden of cost. One thing worse than a rash, is a rash you also paid for.

Unfortunately, society (read liberal media) has given pharmaceutical representatives a bum rap. Too often they are depicted as a bunch of used car salesmen (no offence meant to those patients of mine who practice that for a living) who lure physicians into using bad, harmful drugs that probably cause liver failure and death to innocent patients. All the while, they are sporting doctors off to vacation rendezvous with naked women and plenty of booze. That couldn't be further from the truth. These women are not usually naked. Has that ever happened? I am sure it has. I saw it at the movies also with Dr. Richard Kimble and the one armed man. But I personally have yet to see a one armed pharmaceutical rep. And believe me, I am on the lookout.

Other than occasionally being guilty of annoying the hell out of us by being too pushy while we are trying to see patients, they are only trying to sell a new drug that is usually better than the other ones we've been using. It may be easier to take; it may be more potent; it may have fewer side effects than others. What's so wrong with that? Chrysler, Cadillac, Sony, and Proctor & Gamble representatives all do the same thing. This is capitalism at its best and it has made America the envy of the world in medicine and pharmaceuticals. In the process, they are also guilty of educating the physicians on drugs and ideas that weren't even available when we went to medical school. And if they didn't, I am suddenly out of date. Do you want your physician using medicines from the 1800s when there may be something better that was developed a year ago? Frankly, I know I don't.

Pharmaceutical reps are well educated also. Almost all of them have a college degree and most of them majored in the sciences. Could you have mastered that curriculum? They don't just give those degrees away, you know. They are able to speak intelligently about more biochemistry than I usually want to know or care to remember and they are far above the charlatan snake oil salesmen, as they are often depicted.

I once walked out of an exam room and found a couple of pharmaceutical representatives waiting for me in their usual place out in the hall. Sartoriously dressed and professionally polite, they waited for me to finish giving instructions to my nursing staff on the patient I had just seen. They needed to grab a quick signature for medicine samples, educate me for just a moment in that biochemistry stuff I mentioned earlier, and remind me that there was a snack in the break room if I wanted a little something to eat. Recognizing their importance, trying to be understanding of the dilemma they are up against, and wanting to boost my low blood sugar, I attempted to be a little humorous while I entertained them. As I invited them down the hall to my office, I sarcastically said, "Come down here before you drive my patients away. You look like a couple of Mormons."

"Well, one of us is," was the reply. Oops, open mouth, insert foot.

PICA

I believe it was Newman on *Seinfeld* that referred to broccoli as a "vile weed." I often repeat that phrase and George W. Bush and I probably couldn't agree more. Why God made that plant and why someone would think about eating it remains a mystery to me. I bow to His omniscience for the answer to that question. Who am I to question the Almighty? I suppose slugs and lawyers have to eat too. (I am just kidding about the lawyers.)

Craving abnormal foods, however, is different than an abnormal craving for foods. And craving something that is not even food is worse yet. As a physician, I have seen some you wouldn't believe. I remember one lovely lady who came to my office because she had just done something that even she couldn't believe. She had just eaten a box of chalk. That's right, the same white chalk we older peoples' teachers may have used on the chalk board 30 years ago. To those of you who are members of a newer generation, a chalk board was something that hung on the wall in the classroom that was usually black. Your teacher, and sometimes malevolent children like me, would write on it to teach a lesson. Or in my case, I would be found writing "I will not talk when the teacher is talking." This was to teach *me* the lesson of course. And unfortunately, this was written one hundred times after school.

This abnormal craving for ice (pagophagia), dirt (geophagia), or in this instance, chalk (chalkophagia), is what we physicians call a sign. And it usually means one thing: iron deficiency anemia. The mechanism by which all this occurs is unknown. Well, at least, it is unknown to me. I am sure there are those who know the true answer. Maybe you were not loved as a child or your parents abused you by making you clean your room. Or maybe you have been exposed to too much carbon dioxide through global warming. Either way, it is usually cured by simply taking iron supplements to replete your low iron storage.

So let me give you some advice. If you find yourself eating chalk or excessive ice or dirt or something just as bad, come see me. If you find yourself eating broccoli, just don't sit next to me at the dinner table.

Picture Perfect

eaders Digest used to have a section called "Humor in Medicine." It may still. I rarely read it anymore since apparently what I see as humor couldn't ever pass their editor as being funny enough to put into print. No bitterness really, just a statement of fact. It could be that some stories are better told than relayed through print. I will let you decide. Stories are always a little more funny if you have had too much to drink. So sit down, take another sip. The retelling of this office incident has always kept my partners in stitches. Not literally of course.

Performing flexible sigmoidoscopies is more of something from the past. Not way past as Scrooge's ghost may say, but your past. In recent memory, it became just as easy to do an entire colonoscopy rather than just stopping at the half-way point. And with the insurance and government agencies drastically decreasing payment for services, it became impractical to spend office time for the procedure. So now we just send everybody to the Gastroenterologist or a General Surgeon to get the whole nine yards, literally.

One of my last performances navigating the "Hershey Highway" as I have heard it called behind closed doors, or at least while the patient is supposedly sedated, was one to remember. And thank the Lord; it was done in the presence of a physician's assistant in training who fortunately had a sick sense of humor that matched my nurse's and my own. This can get dangerous.

It all began a long time ago in a land far, far away…The proper way to start a sigmoidoscopy, after getting verbal consent from the patient of course, is to "sweep the rectum" with a gloved finger. Gloved is the key word here. This allows you to either detect any tumors at the rectal verge that could get missed by the scope or it gives your nurse time to figure out why the damn suction isn't working again.

This procedure began in the usual way except it was complicated by his size. Weighing in at a robust 300 pounds (I may be exaggerating a pound or two) made his butt cheeks, I mean gluteus maximums, well, maximums. As Dr. Frankenstein would say, "That goes without saying." This not only complicated the rectal sweep, as I could barely get my hand far enough to even get my finger poised and positioned for the necessary action, I couldn't even engage the scope. And that caused "the rest of the story," as Paul Harvey would have said.

When it was time to now peer down the monocular scope to begin navigation of the bowel, rather than seeing the rectum, all I saw was the face of the prettiest nurse on the planet. My first thought was that she had been swallowed up after standing too close to this gigantic hole. I yelled for her to get out of there and reached to grab her hand to pull her out. You can imagine my relief when I realized that the scope hadn't actually made it into the rectum as planned. Instead, it had curled up in those large butt cheeks I mentioned earlier and was now pointing back at my nurse who was seated right beside me instead of down the passageway of no return. Try experiencing that with a straight face. Of course my nurse and the physician's assistant raced out of the room, laughing hysterically, while I was left to make up something for the patient to ponder while all three of us regained our exposure to finish the exam. I guess that's why I get paid the big bucks. Hey, maybe that editor of *Reader's Digest* was the patient. Oh well, all is well that ends well.

Kids, Say the Cutest Things

One of the decisions you have to make after completing your first four years of medical school is what area of medicine you are going to make your profession. Are you squeamish about blood? You shouldn't choose surgery. Do you like only scheduled hours and shift work? You may want to consider being an emergency room physician. Are you okay with variety in patient ages, gender and disease states? Consider family medicine. Have you considered being a pediatrician? How do you do with children? Or even more importantly, how do you do with the parents of the little gems? Do you want your patients to ever get well? Don't choose dermatology.

This is one of the reasons *I* chose family medicine. Variety? Throw it at me. I have gone from the death bed to the delivery room in a matter of minutes. I have jumped from examining an aging senior citizen to a squealing newborn. That's okay too. Well, it was actually the newborn's parents squealing because I was running a little late that day. Gender? I have gone from male to female to I'm-not-sure-what-was-in-room-number-three. Squeamish? I'll have none of that in my office. Why, I've opened an abscess with one hand and started eating lunch with the other. What fun! Just don't forget which hand is gloved.

But one of the things I like the most about family medicine is those darn kids. They can really make my day. I personally don't want to see them all day long like a pediatrician may, but a few each day is okay with me.

An older physician friend passed down a set of magnifying goggles to me as I began my practice. He had used the very same ones to look at rashes up close or to suture the very fine work that often needs to be done. They are indispensable. He told me a kid asked him as he donned these goggles, "Are you going to weld me?" What fun! They actually do look just like a small pair of welding goggles.

One of my own personal encounters that made me laugh was with a very cute and precocious little girl of about four years of age. She had unfortunately developed a case of Streptococcal pharyngitis. The poor little thing. She was not toxic but certainly having a bad day. Of course, as you learn to treat this disease, you remember that it is one we tend to worry about. It isn't just a sore throat because it can progress into Scarlet fever, Rheumatic fever, a peritonsillar abscess (this is what I understand killed "the Gipper"), and post-streptococcal renal failure. It is important to treat Strept throat aggressively and completely. That means actually finishing your course of antibiotics rather than letting them sit on the shelf after you start feeling a little better. Also, we are careful to isolate the child so as not to spread it readily to their siblings—or their doctor.

Upon hearing that she needed to be put in isolation for 24 hours while the antibiotics did their stuff, and apparently assuming that isolation meant solitary confinement where she would be slipped food through a crack under the door, she grew a sad little face, looked pitifully up at me and said, "I am going to be a very lonely girl." Now isn't that the cutest thing you heard today?

Pregnant?

One of the greatest things about being a Family Medicine physician is participating in the actual *planning* of a family. Many couples come to the physician wanting to start their family and looking for advice. We often get to counsel young women on nutrition, physical exercise, and other aspects to make their pregnancy and birthing experience a little a better.

One of the happiest times in the office is when you actually get to read the pregnancy test result to the expectant mother. To see their face light up and begin that glow that all pregnant women are famous for is truly a delight.

One such incident occurred in my office just a few months ago. In the bustle of jumping from one room to another, stamping out disease here and stamping out disease there, my nurse handed me a third "positive test." Amazing! I had just had two pregnancies confirmed in a row. The first was in room one and the second in room two. Now, she handed me a positive lab result for room three and told me, "Wow, three positives in a row."

I bounded into the room full of excitement and happy to tell the young mother that she was pregnant. We all had a laugh when she just looked at me and said, "Really? I just came in with a sore throat." The lab test was positive alright but it was one box higher in the "Rapid Strept Test" slot and not in the slot for the "Pregnancy Test."

Let's Play Ball!

Every once in a while a physician feels their worth. That's right. I am not always saving lives or stamping out disease. Sometimes when I am on call, my wife can hear me giving instructions to the worried patient over the telephone. It usually goes something like this, "Now, have you tried prune juice or any other over-the-counter laxatives?" I then get off the phone and say, "Another life saved." What a hero I am. I can make the blind walk, the deaf see, and the lame hear—or something like that.

Bob walked into my office one morning for a complete physical. As with most men, he was there because his wife told him to be there. Men only come in to see a physician on their own when something is wrong in their major organ system, the genitals. And not just something wrong, it has to be really wrong. If that part is working, they can tolerate just about anything. And even when the genitals are just limping along, they avoid the physician with a few months of simple neglect. I cannot even count the number of testicles I have seen that are as large as a baseball to which their owners shamefully admit, "It's been this way for about 6 months." Amazing!

Bob didn't have a testicle enlarged at all. Worse, the enlargement was right there on his face. Yes, right there on his face was an abscessed pore that had grown to be the size of a baseball. I am not exaggerating here. And amazingly, he didn't ask anything about it. I did my usual physical exam covering everything from head to toe, past medical history, current medical concerns, but nothing was mentioned of this huge facial mass. Nothing. I was surprised that he didn't have a "baby on board" sign hanging off of it. I was dodging getting hit by the thing every time he turned his head to the left or right.

Finally, I had to ask, (unable to avoid the elephant in the room any longer.) "Hey, Bob, what is this thing on your face?" He replied that it had been there for about ten years. That's right, *YEARS!* And he had done nothing about it. Did he think that no one noticed? Had none of his close friends had the courtesy to give him advice to at least visit his physician to get a second opinion?

I told Bob that I wasn't a plastic surgeon but I would love to take a stab (not literally, but sort of) at cleaning this thing up for him, *TODAY!* He was surprisingly willing for me to proceed without a second opinion. But then again, what did he have to lose? It couldn't get any worse. I told him that I would like to anesthetize it a little, and then drain it with a small incision that he wouldn't feel. I would then inject a little steroid into what tissue remained and thought that it would scar down pretty well. I wouldn't have done this in a pretty young woman but he had nothing to lose, I assure you. After a relatively short time, say a half an hour, he was a new man. The abscess was easily drained of about a cup of sebaceous pus and a little blood. Unfortunately, my nurse assistant walked in right as the dam burst and wouldn't eat the cream of mushroom soup I had offered to buy her for lunch that day. Other than that, all went well.

I was fortunate to see him back a few times and remained amazed at how nicely his face turned out. The gratitude expressed by him and his wife on subsequent visits has always been so very rewarding. I was worth my salt that day.

Never Assume Anything

While you are home sleeping, your doctor may not be. He may be up answering phone calls. Doctors often share "call" with their partners, covering the fact that not everyone gets sick during the daytime. How inappropriate is that? Again, how many babies are born between 9am and 5pm? Right, not so many. You understand the problem. Call is the answer.

One of the special problems associated with practicing medicine over the telephone is the person on the other end. I know what I mean when I say "hemorrhage," but what do *you* mean when you say "hemorrhage?" A little bit of pink on the toilet paper after you wipe your bottom is not a hemorrhage to me. Likewise, when you have been changing tampons every two minutes because the blood just keeps on coming, you may need to see someone face-to-face. Or at least bottom to face, if you know what I mean.

One physician told me of a time when a new mother called to tell him that she felt her baby wasn't getting enough milk to drink. This is not an unusual problem. He told her that a simple remedy would be to take a large sewing needle and heat it up on the stove to make it red-hot. Then stick the needle down the tip of the nipple to widen the port where the milk comes out. Sounds easy enough, doesn't it? Now back to sleep.

Another phone call a few minutes later from the same concerned mother explains the real problem. "Isn't that going to hurt?" He didn't realize that she was breast feeding. Ouch!

Whew, That Was Close

You shouldn't fool with medicines. They are dangerous. Not just some, but all. Let's take coumadin, for example. Medicare doesn't pay for physicians to manage coumadin therapy. This is a horrible decision made by some panel of idiots who don't understand the consequences of their decision. Coumadin, for those of you that are not in the know, is used to thin the blood and prevent embolic events in certain diseases. Two classic examples are DVTs –deep venous thrombosis—which are clots that form in the legs and can break off and go to your lungs causing pulmonary embolisms, and unfortunately, sudden death. Another example is atrial-fibrillation, which is an abnormal heart condition that can lead to embolisms that can go to the brain causing strokes. Both of these are bad.

Coumadin, itself, is rat poison. It is also known as warfarin. We put it in pill form, of course, so we can control the dosage and give it in just the right amount. Too little and you remain at risk for the above. Too much and you are now at risk for a hemorrhagic stroke, which is much worse. Patients need to be monitored at least monthly. Otherwise, they may end up on the floor of the garage, just like that rat who didn't take the right amount. Why the government doesn't pay for this is simple, they don't care. It's apparently better to save a few dollars here and there regardless of the outcome.

Even under the best circumstances, things can go wrong when administering medicines. I remember one event that occurred on my first day of call. I had rounded at the hospital that morning with the medicine team. They introduced me to a man named Mr. Jones who was being treated for a severe pneumonia. He was in grave condition, at one time, but we had isolated the organism that was causing the infection and I was informed that he was "turning around." Yeah for modern medicine and pharmacology. I was surprised a few hours later, when I was called to the hospital by a nurse who informed me that Mr. Jones "was leaving." I didn't know where he would be going since, although I knew he was apparently getting better, I had no intention of sending him home just yet. "No," the nurse informed me, "he is dying." Now I was really surprised.

I ran over to the hospital to find Mr. Jones surrounded by his extended family. They were all saying their goodbyes in a very touching manner that would have moved the coldest heart. It moved mine too. It moved me to call the attending physician and find out what the heck was going on. I was under the assumption that he was doing better. My attending physician asked me what his respiratory rate was. "About 5 per minute," I said. He then asked me what I thought my respiratory rate would be if I had pneumonia and struggling to breathe. I correctly answered back, for probably the first time in my young medical career, "About 50."

It seems that the nurse was so eager to make sure that Mr. Jones was comfortable that she was giving morphine to him like candy to a kid at the county fair. Morphine makes you comfortable, alright, but it also is a respiratory depressant. The physician had written the order for morphine to be given every hour PRN (as needed). Pretty soon he would be comfortable, alright. He would be taking harp lessons in the heavenly symphony.

Now, a miracle was about to occur. Let me introduce a medicine called Narcan. This medicine reverses the effects of morphine and other narcotics—in about three minutes. I am especially thankful that the attending physician told me this. After explaining to the family that I thought I could help him breathe a little better and that I was going to adjust his medicine regime, I administered the Narcan. I then stepped out of the room and waited so as not to have to accept worship when Mr. Jones woke up. And wake up, he did. Within a few minutes he was sitting up, requesting food, and enjoying his extended family once again. Whew, that was close.

Specialists and Generalists

They say that doctors can be divided into two basic disciplines, those who practice as specialists and those who practice generalized medicine. Generalized medicine includes Pediatrics, Family Medicine, and Internal Medicine. The specialists are basically all the rest.

On a more basic level, we who practice generalized medicine say that the specialists study to learn everything about only one field of study. They eventually know so much about so little that they know practically everything about nothing. The specialists on the other hand say that we generalists study to know a little about all fields of study. Eventually we know practically nothing about everything. Both are probably right.

For example, I was taking care of a patient of mine who had suffered a myocardial infarction (a heart attack). Due to his advanced age, it was decided that surgical intervention was not appropriate and that medical therapy with cardiac medicines was the treatment of preference. But I was unsure how long we needed to keep him in the hospital under observation as he recovered. Finally, after much anxiety about having to ask a cardiologist what seemed like such a stupid question, I put aside my pride and asked the cardiac specialist what he would suggest? He nicely told me that typically it would be about three days in order to monitor for cardiac arrhythmias that could cost him his life. After that, I could safely return the patient to the nursing home where he resided.

Within just a few moments of that physician-to-physician "curbside consult," I noticed that the cardiologist was frantically thumbing through his pocket manual. He was apparently trying to treat a cardiac patient for an acute cystitis (a bladder infection) and was unsure of what medicine to use and how long the therapy should last. Finally, he was able to put aside *his* pride and came over to ask me what I would do. Returning the favor, I nicely informed him of what I thought the best course of treatment would be. We both learned a valuable lesson that day.

Once in a while, a patient seems to have had enough with either discipline altogether. I had one such man come into my office seeking medical advice for anal itching. It seems he had already visited a couple of specialists and all treatment regimens had failed. He had had this problem for more than a year and couldn't take it any longer. His rectum itched all through the night and was keeping him from getting the sleep he so longed for. Being a generalist and knowing practically nothing about everything, I asked him if he had any dogs or cats. "Yes," he informed me. In fact, a few of his dogs road around with him in the pickup truck all day as he cared for his ranch.

To his disgust, I told him that he probably had pinworms. He would eat his lunch, pet the dogs, and continue eating. A classic set up if you ask me. I gave him a prescription for Vermox. One pill, taken today, and his itching would be cured, if I was correct in my diagnosis. That's it.

I was so pleased when he returned in a couple of weeks to inform me how grateful he was to have been cured. He was only angry that he had spent all this time and money seeing various specialists who ran test after test with no results. I guess it helps to occasionally know so little about everything, as long as you know the one thing that helps. And he'll never eat around his dogs again, that's for sure.

Now That's a Memory!

They say that an elephant has a great memory. How scientists have determined that, I don't even know. Were they asked to memorize the fifty states and their capital cities and then questioned on it later? I don't think so. Perhaps it's just one of those "wives' tales" and we all know how those can be. One person that I know who has a great memory is not an elephant at all, although you couldn't over look him in the room—if you know what I mean.

Cornelius Ross, MD was one of my professors at medical school. He was the chairman of the department of Anatomy at the University of Washington, School of Medicine and our instructor of gross anatomy. Now you may think that all anatomy is gross as you dissect a human cadaver. But the phrase "gross anatomy" refers to the discipline of dissecting the torso and the major human organs and is not to be confused with the "head and neck" anatomy or the "musculoskeletal" portions. Those classes follow in successive semesters. A movie by the same name was produced in 1989 and it was accurate enough to bring the hairs on the back of my neck to a stand. It truly depicted the fact that even though the 6 credit class was a small portion of your first semester curriculum, it occupied about 70% of your time for study. Countless hours were spent teasing out every organ, muscle, nerve, artery and vein. And believe me; you had better know them all.

Dr. Ross met us on the first day of medical school. Eight sharp! Our pictures, however, had arrived three days earlier. We had arrived to begin an orientation on Thursday, had our pictures quickly taken, like criminals being booked at the county jail, and were carted off to begin learning how to work together as a team. Dr. Ross had apparently been waiting for this to happen.

Monday morning, the first day of medical school came soon enough. I remember arriving about 15 minutes early and found a seat in the large auditorium where over one hundred other medical students, now my colleagues, were gathering. Dr. Ross stood in front of the classroom, dressed in a professional looking white lab coat, a shirt, a tie, and no grin. A few of my classmates arrived a few minutes too late. They would only do this once. Dr. Ross waited patiently until 8:03 AM. Then without a picture or a list, he said, "We have wasted 3 minutes. Sharon, Carl, and Robert, you are late. Tomorrow you will need to take an earlier bus."

He had memorized everyone's name in the class from the pictures taken three days earlier! Now *that* is a memory and he had left an indelible impression on each one of us.

Who Said Life is Fair?

Life isn't fair. Let's get that straight from the start. The same can be said when looking at the inequalities among the health care team. Doctors and nurses are not treated the same. I am not one to advocate that we are equal. Let's not refuse to see the two-ton elephant in the room. I am the one who went to medical school and residency for a total of eleven years. I am the one who pays the malpractice insurance. The buck stops with me, no doubt. But these things don't make me superior in quality as a health care provider or as a person. I can be a jerk or a saint and so can my nurse.

Unfortunately, my nurse gets the worst of my patients while I get most of the glory. For example, when I am running late, some of my patients feel free to complain and gripe to my nurse. They rarely do to me. It's not my job to hide behind that fact nor is it fair to take advantage of this phenomenon. But it does exist. Thank you Lord. I usually fire patients who abuse my nurse because it shows her and my staff that they are important to me, above all else.

However, I did take advantage of this phenomenon to pull a fast one on my first nurse. It was a gem and I am sure you will agree. It was Christmastime, and as usual, the holiday spirit had enticed people and companies to treat me generously as one of their clients. It is not unusual for me to receive a few gifts from nursing homes and patients or from the hospitals, as a sign of appreciation for the work I have sent their way over the year or the service I have given. My wife and I try to do the same to show our appreciation for my nurse and staff.

This particular year, I received a couple of nice gifts to start the Christmas season. I believe one was a nice bottle of wine. The other I don't remember. I do remember that my nurse was feeling a little jealous of the attention I was receiving. Being sensitive to her feelings, *NOT,* I devised a plan. "An absolutely, wonderful, horrible plan," as the Grinch would say. I went home and carefully chose seven nice things that I had received as gifts from years past or things I had actually purchased myself, such as jewelry. I carefully wrapped these in Christmas wrap and addressed them to myself. I then chose seven cheap, thoughtless items such as candy and trinkets and wrapped them in Christmas wrap. These were addressed to my nurse, of course. Then I made sure they were delivered to my office on seven consecutive days right before Christmas. Each day I would receive a wonderful gift and made sure to open it in front of my nurse as she opened her gift, all from fabricated companies and nursing homes.

Each day, her jealousy and envy grew more obvious and each day, I rubbed it in deeper by expounding how wonderful my new gift was and inquiring about hers. Finally, on our last day before the Christmas break, through much laughter and even a few tears, I revealed to her the joke.

Like a good nurse, she shared my laughter and, of course, eventually got even.

On Call!

Nothing sticks to your craw more than being on call. That word means absolutely nothing to someone who has never done it, and as physicians, we do it every three to four nights for most of our life. It's an onerous responsibility that WE DON'T GET PAID FOR, by the way! It just comes with the job and whether you are fortunate enough to make a lot of money in medicine or whether you are part of the rest that just make a modest income, you still have to do it. It can be a source of angst, and occasionally, it can create a source of another laugh or two. Here is one I remember.

My first night on call as a full fledged, Board Certified, Family Medicine Physician brought some laughter. I had been trained for seven years to treat the sickest people on earth. I mean the people who not only think they are sick, but actually *are* sick! We'll get to those who just *think* they are sick in another series of laughs. They deserve to be laughed at eventually.

I had cared for every patient and disease imaginable and most of them in the ICU (Intensive Care Unit). I saw life and death not only every day but sometimes every hour. This is where a physician earns his stripes and it separates the men from the boys, or equally in medicine today, the ladies from the girls. So when I readied myself for call on my own this night, I thought I was ready for anything.

Then the phone rang. Well, the phone doesn't really ring anymore, as we usually wear a pager as an immediate barrier between the physician and the patient. I love that pager. Anyway, the pager went off and told me which number to call. Take a deep breath, this could be serious, I told myself.

I was able to talk immediately to a wonderful new mother who was sure her little child had contracted Chicken Pox. Her question wasn't one of diagnosis because several of the cousins had just been diagnosed with the same thing. She just wanted to know how to treat its symptoms as it was the weekend and she was unable to ask her personal physician until Monday.

Then this fully fledged, Board Certified, Family Medicine Physician said, "Hold on a minute." I covered the mouth piece a moment and yelled to my wife and mother of three, "Hey, what do you do for Chicken Pox?" My four years of medical school and three years of residency hadn't hurt my wife one bit.

Sleepless in Seattle, And Everywhere Else.

What most people don't understand about the anger, seemingly elicited by the word "call" among physicians, is that it's not the word itself but what it actually implies, i.e. lack of sleep. If you don't think losing sleep is a big deal then you need to spend a few nights with me. If you were just to stay up and watch television or do work on your "honey do list," it would be okay. "Hey, no problem calling; I'm up working outside on my deck anyway. How can I help you?" The problem lies in the continuous effort to stay asleep while the pager keeps going off every hour or two, sometimes every minute or two. And don't even *think* about actually staying up and beating the system because then the pager will never go off. It's just one of Murphy's Laws in the universe.

So this is what you are facing when as a patient you make that decision late in the night to call your physician. Please give some thought before you do. Remember, their attitude toward all the patients they see in the office tomorrow may be affected by your decision. It may determine whether that man gets a digital rectal exam or a pass to just go home. It determines whether they use any anesthesia when they incise and drain that minor abscess or whether they just "go for it." Ask yourself again, **can this wait until tomorrow after sun up?** Please! And, thank you!

I received a call about 2 AM once from a mother that was concerned about her young daughter's foot. Apparently, the child had complained earlier in the day about her foot hurting. However, according to mom there had been no known trauma. "What should I do about it?" she asked.

"Well, I said, what does it look like? Is it red or swollen? Are there any signs of trauma such as a puncture or sore?"

"I don't know," she said, "I haven't looked at it."

You have a daughter who complains about a sore foot all day and you never looked at it? "Well, why don't you take a look and see for me before we go any further—down this possibly endless highway."

"She's asleep and I don't want to wake her."

So again, at two in the morning you called me and you *haven't even looked at it?* And it's bothering her so much that *she's fast asleep?* And you woke me up at *two in the morning* about this?

Every male in the office got a rectal exam that day, even my nursing assistant.

Okinawa

During the first year of medical school, it is important to learn the basic skills of being a human being. Although this may seem to be a needless step, as many of you already know, apparently not every doctor was in attendance for that class. This training usually begins with the process of learning basic interviewing skills. As medical schools are always looking for ways of saving money, they incorporate the cheapest methods of obtaining appropriate bodies—I mean patients. It is no wonder that they obtained the reputation of stealing bodies from the cemeteries in the dark of night. They did. Well, actually they paid people under the table to do the dirty work for them. "It could be worse. It could be raining," as Igor would have said. Where I went to medical school, instead of stooping to that, we were just sent to the Veteran's Hospital. There is nothing like a hospital full of feisty, old veterans that are sitting around shooting the bull to use as interviewees.

Peter and I were sent to the surgical floor. No one there was really too sick. Most of them were suffering from the effects of a sixty-pack-a-year history of smoking rather than any real war wounds. And many of them had no surgery date even scheduled yet. You could say that they were on "standby." As soon as there were no more *real* surgical patients left, they would then choose one these guys and finally fix that hernia they had been worried about for the past seven months. As they had nothing better to do, they gladly submitted to an interview or two. Someone would now listen to their stories even if they had to be paid, or rather, would pay to do it. That's called tuition and books.

As the interview began, I was far less nervous than the other medical student only because I was about ten years older. Interviewing people was not new for me so I sat back and let him go first. Peter had done his homework and worked efficiently as he proceeded from past surgical history, to past medical history, to current medications, to known medicine allergies, and then right in to a good social history. Peter was gaining momentum as he inquired whether the veteran had done any traveling during his long stay upon this earth. I was just along for the ride watching Peter skate along smoothly, until Peter slipped on the ice and nearly broke his neck—so to speak.

The veteran had stated that, yes, he indeed had done a little traveling. He had spent some time on an island called Okinawa, Japan. My jaw dropped immediately when Peter then asked him if he had a summer home there.

"Summer home?" The veteran fired back. "I was fighting a F*&#ING war you idiot!"

Oh how soon we seem to forget from one generation to the next. As they say, if there is one thing we learn from history, it's that we don't learn from history. I quickly helped Peter escape before the paralysis of a *real* broken neck set in.

Slipped Femoral Capital Epiphysis

I am a miracle worker. No, really. Just ask a few of my patients who run into my wife at the local grocery store or retail outlet. She has to hold the vomit in her mouth as they expound for thirty minutes on how I practically saved them, or one of their loved ones, from the grave. If it wasn't for the HIPPA law (Health Insurance Portability and Accountability Act), I would tell her the rest of the story about how they were actually just constipated. Instead, I am forced to just accept the worship they cast upon me. It's a burdensome life but somebody has to do it.

The Psalmist said that we are "fearfully and wonderfully made." And yet, unaware of the molecular details of how our bodies were created to fight disease, pump blood and oxygen from one part to another, or produce energy through mitochondria at the cellular level, he was truly right. And most importantly, he was giving credit where credit was due. He was worshiping the Creator of this great feat of engineering called the human body.

Admittedly, as physicians, we get credit for what God does all the time. Many of the aliments we suffer with, from one day to the next, are completely self-limited. In fact, one of the adages we have in medicine is that when someone calls in sick, you had better get them in to see you right away before they get better all by themselves. Occasionally, we do actually get to use some of that medical training we spent years learning. And, to keep our medical licenses, we have to complete 50 hours of continuing medical education for each year we are in practice. We wouldn't want all that to go to waste either, now would we?

Clara was brought in to see me for a sore throat. She had developed a slight fever and complained to her mother one too many times, so an appointment was made. I asked Clara to sit on the examination table so that I could get a better look. It was then that this 10-year-old, prepubescent girl moaned as she lifted her right leg to clear the small step at the end of the exam table. "Oh, that hip has bothered her for over a couple of weeks now," her mother said.

I asked if I could examine Clara a little more thoroughly than just her sore throat. Receiving an okay from the mother, I quickly went to work and did an x-ray to confirm my suspicions. There it was. Before me was what I would diagnose as a slipped femoral capital epiphysis. More common in prepubescent children who are also a little overweight, the cap of the femoral hip bone slips off the femur head at the growth plate, just like a scoop of ice cream slips off the cone when held by a careless child. She went to surgery within 24 hours so as to keep her from becoming a life-long cripple.

The Orthopedic surgeon was impressed that I was able to make this rare diagnosis. Well, I should be able to. I just read an excellent medical article about it the night before her office visit. Isn't God great?!

Christmas Cheer

Before I ever became a physician, I was a clinical administrator for a group of primary care physicians who knew little to nothing about business themselves. Most physicians don't know a thing about the practice of business and it often shows in their administrative decisions. Unfortunately, they don't teach business principles during your medical school rotations. Most physicians have never even worked for someone longer than a few weeks in their short lives, let alone long enough to have developed any skills as a business owner or employer. They unfortunately go from high school to college to medical school to employer and skip those important steps.

I was fortunate enough to be able to do both. Well, actually, I wasn't smart enough to get into medical school the first time I applied so I was forced to learn business the hard way. It was called the school of hard knocks. I started as a paperboy at 12 years of age and the rest just happened. One thing I understood from the beginning was the value of service and the importance of collecting money for those services. In business, these two are always the most important.

After these two, comes the art of getting the right people to work for you and retaining them through proper appreciation and motivation. One thing I incorporated with that purpose in mind, was an annual cookie bakeoff during the Christmas season. Designed to provide camaraderie among the staff, each person was directed to bring a dozen cookies that would be entered in the contest. The physicians would be the judges. As the manager, I would simply provide the prize monies. One hundred dollars of extra Christmas money would be given for the grand prize, while lesser amounts were used for second and third place finishes.

Enter contestant—and employee—Vivian. Vivian was one of the best workers we had. But she was not an enthusiast when it came to using the kitchen. She had one only because it came with the house. Although I am sure she would have liked the prize money, we had to reject her entry when she presented a beautifully displayed tray of— Oreo cookies. You have to give her credit for imagination.

The Sweet Smell of Success

Most people don't know what the olfactory bulb is or, for that matter, that they even have one. They appreciate that they do, however, when they take a whiff of those odors that conjure up fond or not-so-fond memories from our distant past. Consider the smell of a skunk that sends us scurrying away from disaster or the smell of bacon frying and coffee brewing over an open fire from our childhood days of camping in the great outdoors.

One smell that brings back memories to many of us guys is analgesic balm. Just the thought of it brings back a memory of when some fellow student (read jerk) with a sick sense of humor rubbed it into a few jock straps in physical education class back in junior high. I know it was junior high because where I come from, if it was high school, he'd be dead. It burned forever—yes, I mean that as a pun—into the hippocampus portion of the brain where our memories are usually stored. You will never hear one of *us* ask, "Is that analgesic balm I smell?" We know it is!

Barbara came to my office with low back pain. She was worried about her kidneys. Most people fail to remember that the kidneys are located *high* in the back, just under the rib cage. As one of the most important organs, the good Lord knew better than to place them lower in the back where they would get kicked, beaten and damaged. He used the ribs as a protective barrier just as we would expect an omniscient God to do.

Barbara had been lifting boxes, pushing filing cabinets, or pulling weeds and was feeling the muscles in her lower back as they complained about the strenuous work they had been doing. There was little I could do except to reassure her that her kidneys were fine and that her application of the analgesic balm already in place was a good procedure.

"Analgesic balm?" She retorted. That smell happened to be a new perfume she had just purchased at more than $70.00 an ounce.

Oops. Maybe *my* olfactory bulb was burned a little deeper than I thought.

Talk About Nuts

During my first clinical rotation of medical school, I was assigned to the outpatient psychiatric unit at Harborview Medical Center. There, a group of aspiring medical students would pretend to know something about being a physician and interview, as well as attempt to manage, patients who were supposed to have some form of psychiatric illness. That probably only meant that they hadn't quite survived the medical school rigors as clearly as I had.

My first day started quickly when we couldn't even ride the elevator to the fourth floor because one of the patients kept pushing the "open door" button each time the door got close to actually closing. We literally had to pull her back and restrain her at the back of the elevator in order to get going. *Her* elevator obviously never went to the top floor.

One of my first patients was a man who apparently suffered from "illusions of grandeur." In other words, he thought that he was far more important than he actually was, or in this case, maybe more important than *we* thought he was. Anyway, I was informed that this man thought that he "knew" Princess Diana. I couldn't wait to interview him.

"So I hear that you know Princess Diana," I started.

He quickly denied that, but did admit that he had received a letter from her once. He then explained that he had been an occasional financial contributor to an orphanage that both she and Prince Charles had encouraged. After contributing regular sums of money, he regretted that he had never even received a thank you for his efforts. He had written to them and explained that if his money wasn't appreciated, he would instead be contributing to another area of need. Subsequently, said letter was received and his apparent illusion of grandeur gained seed and his diagnosis confirmed. He sounded nuts to me.

"So, do you have this letter so I can see it," I asked questionably.

"It is in a safe, you idiot. Would you be carrying her letter around if you had received it?"

He had a great point there. Now I am not sure *who* had the illusions of grandeur, the patient or the physicians who were directing the unit.

About Dr. Edgerly

This is not my real picture any more than Engelbert Humperdinck's real name was, well, Engelbert Humperdinck. Who would ever let their child be named Engelbert Humperdinck? In looking at the cartoon, however, the similarities with my real picture are remarkable. I didn't use my real picture because this one actually looks better than any other one I've taken. How many of us show off our driver's license? Right, you get the picture!?

In the past, I have also written under the pseudonym of Dr. Strangeglove and, of course, that wasn't my real name either. Dr. Strangeglove was a pseudonym to protect, not the innocent, but actually the guilty (me). In today's world, where there is a lawyer on every corner, I felt that I needed all the protection I could get. I am a real doctor; however, I never really played one on television—at least not yet.

I practice medicine (and I mean *practice*) in rural Eastern Washington State, not D.C. If you're ever in the area, I invite you to get sick and drop in.

And, if you enjoy this book, I invite you to waste more of your precious time on my blog at Doctorstrangeglove.com or richardedgerlymd.com. Go for it.

Richard Edgerly, MD